THE KINGFISHER BOOK OF
NURSERY RHYMES
AND
LULLABIES

ILLUSTRATED BY HILDA OFFEN

KINGFISHER BOOKS

For Lorraine

First published in this edition in 1987
by Kingfisher Books Limited, Elsley Court,
20–22 Great Titchfield Street, London W1P 7AD.
A Grisewood & Dempsey Company.
Some of the illustrations in this book are taken
from a *Treasury of Nursery Rhymes* (1984)
and *Lullabies* (1986).

BRITISH CATALOGUING IN PUBLICATION DATA
Nursery rhymes & lullabies
1. Nursery rhymes, English
I. Offen, Hilda
398'.8   PZ8.3
ISBN: 0 86272 222 5

Edited by Vanessa Clarke
Designed by Denise Gardner
Cover designed by Pinpoint Design Company
Phototypeset by Tradespools Ltd., Frome, Somerset
Colour separations by Newsele Litho, Milan
Printed by Vallardi Industrie Grafiche, Milan

OLD MOTHER GOOSE

Old Mother Goose,
　　When she wanted to wander,
Would ride through the air
　　On a very fine gander.

Mother Goose had a house,
　　'Twas built in a wood,
Where an owl at the door
　　For sentinel stood.

She had a son Jack,
   A plain-looking lad,
He was not very good,
   Nor yet very bad.

She sent him to market,
   A live goose he bought;
See, mother, says he,
   I have not been for nought.

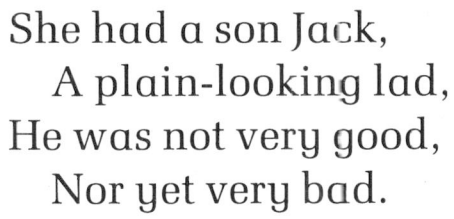

Jack's goose and her gander
   Grew very fond;
They'd both eat together,
   Or swim in the pond.

Jack found one fine morning,
As I have been told,
His goose had laid him
An egg of pure gold.

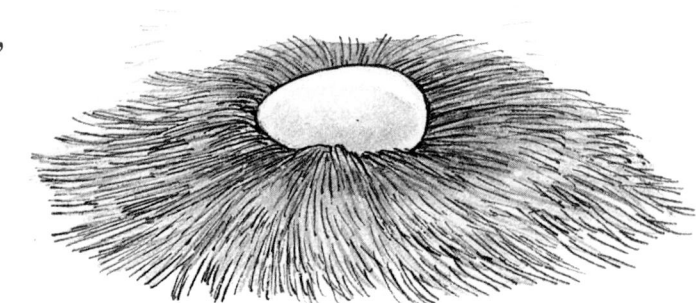

Jack ran to his mother
The news for to tell,
She called him a good boy,
And said it was well.

Jack sold his gold egg
To a merchant untrue,
Who cheated him out of
A half of his due.

Then Jack went a-courting
    A lady so gay,
As fair as the lily,
    And sweet as the May.

The merchant and squire
    Soon came at his back
And began to belabour
    The sides of poor Jack.

Then old Mother Goose
    That instant came in,
And turned her son Jack
    Into famed Harlequin.

A WEEK OF BIRTHDAYS

Monday's child is fair of face,
Tuesday's child is full of grace,
Wednesday's child is full of woe,
Thursday's child has far to go,
Friday's child is loving and giving,
Saturday's child works hard for its living,
And the child that's born on the Sabbath day
Is bonny and blithe, and good and gay.

GIRLS AND BOYS COME
OUT TO PLAY

Girls and boys come out to play,
The moon doth shine as bright as day.
Leave your supper and leave your sleep,
And come with your playfellows into the street.
Come with a whoop and come with a call,
Come with a good will or not at all.
Up the ladder and down the wall,
A half-penny loaf will serve us all;
You find milk, and I'll find flour,
And we'll have a pudding in half an hour.

TO THE BAT

Bat, bat, come under my hat,
   And I'll give you a slice of bacon;
And when I bake, I'll give you a cake,
   If I am not mistaken.

HIGGLETY, PIGGLETY

Higglety, pigglety, pop!
The dog has eaten the mop;
   The pig's in a hurry,
   The cat's in a flurry,
Higglety, pigglety, pop!

THE FLYING PIG

Dickery, dickery, dare,
The pig flew up in the air;
The man in brown
Soon brought him down,
Dickery, dickery, dare.

THREE GHOSTESSES

Three little ghostesses,
Sitting on postesses,
Eating buttered toastesses,
Greasing their fistesses,
Up to their wristesses.
Oh, what beastesses
To make such feastesses!

HICKORY,
DICKORY,
DOCK

Hickory, dickory, dock,
The mouse ran up the clock.
  The clock struck one,
  The mouse ran down,
Hickory, dickory, dock.

THE MISCHIEVOUS RAVEN

A farmer went trotting upon his grey mare,
    Bumpety, bumpety, bump!
With his daughter behind him so rosy and fair,
    Lumpety, lumpety, lump!

A raven cried, Croak! and they all tumbled down,
    Bumpety, bumpety, bump!
The mare broke her knees and the farmer his crown,
    Lumpety, lumpety, lump!

The mischievous raven flew laughing away,
    Bumpety, bumpety, bump!
And vowed he would serve them the same the next day,
    Lumpety, lumpety, lump!

THREE BLIND MICE

Three blind mice, see how they run!
They all ran after the farmer's wife,
Who cut off their tails with a carving knife,
Did you ever see such a thing in your life,
    As three blind mice?

DAVY DUMPLING

Davy Davy Dumpling,
Boil him in the pot;
Sugar him and butter him,
And eat him while he's hot.

THE KILKENNY CATS

There were once two cats of Kilkenny,
Each thought there was one cat too many;
So they fought and they fit,
And they scratched and they bit,
    Till, excepting their nails,
    And the tips of their tails,
Instead of two cats, there weren't any.

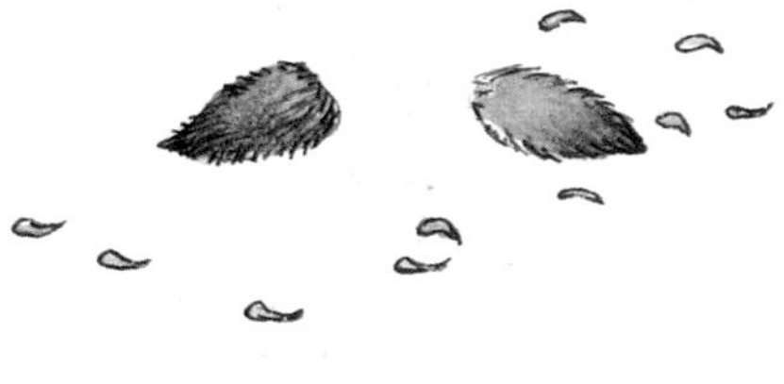

THE CUCKOO

Cuckoo, cuckoo, what do you do?
In April I open my bill;
In May I sing all day;
In June I change my tune;
In July I prepare to fly;
In August away I must.

OLD MOTHER HUBBARD

Old Mother Hubbard
Went to her cupboard,
To fetch her poor dog a bone;
But when she got there
The cupboard was bare
And so the poor dog had none.

She went to the baker's
To buy him some bread;
But when she came back
The poor dog was dead.

She went to the joiner's
To buy him a coffin;
But when she came back
The poor dog was laughing.

She took a clean dish
   To get him some tripe;
But when she came back
   He was smoking a pipe.

She went to the fishmonger's
   To buy him some fish;
But when she came back
   He was licking the dish.

She went to the tavern
   For white wine and red;
But when she came back
   The dog stood on his head.

She went to the fruiterer's
   To buy him some fruit;
But when she came back
   He was playing the flute.

She went to the tailor's
   To buy him a coat;
But when she came back
   He was riding a goat.

She went to the hatter's
   To buy him a hat;
But when she came back
   He was feeding the cat.

She went to the barber's
   To buy him a wig;
But when she came back
   He was dancing a jig.

She went to the cobbler's
   To buy him some shoes;
But when she came back
   He was reading the news.

She went to the seamstress
   To buy him some linen;
But when she came back
   The dog was a-spinning.

She went to the hosier's
   To buy him some hose;
But when she came back
   He was dressed in his clothes.

The dame made a curtsey,
   The dog made a bow;
The dame said, "Your servant,"
   The dog said, "Bow-wow."

SOLOMON GRUNDY

Solomon Grundy,
Born on a Monday,
Christened on Tuesday,
Married on Wednesday,
Took ill on Thursday,
Worse on Friday,
Died on Saturday,
Buried on Sunday.
This is the end
Of Solomon Grundy.

POP GOES THE WEASEL!

Up and down the City Road,
  In and out the Eagle,
That's the way the money goes,
  Pop goes the weasel!

Half a pound of tuppeny rice,
  Half a pound of treacle,
Mix it up and make it nice,
  Pop goes the weasel!

Every night when I go out
  The monkey's on the table;
Take a stick and knock it off,
  Pop goes the weasel!

JEREMIAH

Jeremiah, blow the fire,
  Puff, puff, puff!
First you blow it gently,
  Then you blow it rough.

ON SATURDAY NIGHT

On Saturday night I lost my wife,
And where do you think I found her?
Up in the moon, singing a tune,
And all the stars around her.

PUSSY CAT MEW

Pussy cat mew jumped over a coal,
And in her best petticoat burned a great hole;
Pussy cat mew shall have no more milk,
Until her best petticoat's mended with silk.

IT'S RAINING

It's raining, it's pouring,
The old man's snoring;
He got into bed
And bumped his head
And couldn't get up in
    the morning.

JINGLE BELLS

Jingle, bells! Jingle, bells!
    Jingle all the way;
Oh, what fun it is to ride
    In a one-horse open sleigh.

QUEEN CAROLINE

Queen, Queen Caroline,
Washed her hair in turpentine,
Turpentine to make it shine,
Queen, Queen Caroline.

ALPHABET PIE

A was an
Apple pie

B
Bit it

C
Cut it

D
Dealt it

E
Eat it

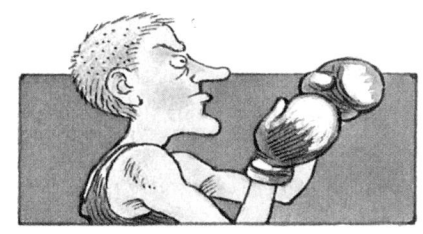

F
Fought for it

G
Got it

H
Had it

I
Inspected it

J
Jumped for it

K
Kept it

L
Longed for it

M
Mourned for it

N
Nodded at it

O
Opened it

P
Peeped in it

Q
Quartered it

R
Ran for it

S
Stole it

T
Took it

U
Upset it

V
Viewed it

W
Wanted it

XYZ & ampersand
All wished for
a piece in hand

DAYS IN THE MONTHS

Thirty days hath September,
April, June, and November;
All the rest have thirty-one.
Excepting February alone,
And that has twenty-eight days clear
And twenty-nine in each leap year.

A MAN IN THE WILDERNESS

A man in the wilderness asked me,
How many strawberries grow in the sea?
I answered him, as I thought good,
As many red herrings as swim in the wood.

PAT-A-CAKE

Pat-a-cake, pat-a-cake, baker's man,
Bake me a cake as fast as you can;
Pat it and prick it, and mark it with B,
Put it in the oven for Baby and me.

THE SKY

Red sky at night,
Shepherd's delight;
Red sky in the morning,
Shepherd's warning.

CONTRARY MARY

Mary, Mary, quite contrary,
  How does your garden grow?
With silver bells and cockle shells,
  And pretty maids all in a row.

LAVENDER'S BLUE

Lavender's blue, dilly, dilly,
   Lavender's green,
When I am king, dilly, dilly,
   You shall be queen.

Call up your men, dilly, dilly,
   Set them to work,
Some to the plough, dilly, dilly,
   Some to the cart.

Some to make hay, dilly, dilly,
   Some to thresh corn,
Whilst you and I, dilly, dilly,
   Keep ourselves warm.

JACK AND JILL

Jack and Jill
Went up the hill,
To fetch a pail of water;
Jack fell down,
And broke his crown,
And Jill came tumbling after.

Then up Jack got,
And home did trot,
As fast as he could caper;
To old Dame Dob,
Who patched his nob
With vinegar and brown paper.

34

When Jill came in,
How she did grin
To see Jack's paper plaster;
His mother, vexed,
Did whip her next,
For laughing at Jack's disaster.

Now Jack did laugh
And Jill did cry,
But her tears did soon abate;
Then Jill did say,
That they should play
At see-saw across the gate.

BOW-WOW

Bow-wow says the dog,
Mew, mew says the cat,
Grunt, grunt goes the hog,
And squeak goes the rat.

Whoo-oo says the owl,
Caw, caw says the crow,
Quack, quack says the duck,
And what cuckoos say, you know.

36

ONE, TWO, THREE, FOUR, FIVE

One, two, three, four, five,
Once I caught a fish alive,
Six, seven, eight, nine, ten,
Then I let it go again.
Why did you let it go?
Because it bit my finger so.
Which finger did it bite?
The little finger on the right.

MOSES

Moses supposes his toeses are roses,
But Moses supposes erroneously;
For nobody's toeses are posies of roses
As Moses supposes his toeses to be.

HUSH, MY BABY

Hush, my baby, do not cry,
Papa's coming by and by;
When he comes he'll come in a gig,
Hi cockalorum, jig, jig, jig.

HUSH THEE

Hush thee, my baby,
Lie still with thy daddy,
Thy mammy has gone to the mill,
To get some meal
To bake a cake,
So pray, my dear baby, lie still.

WILLIE WINKIE

Wee Willie Winkie runs through the town,
Upstairs and downstairs in his nightgown,
Rapping at the window, crying through the lock,
Are all the children in their beds, it's past eight o'clock?

JACK SPRAT

Jack Sprat could eat no fat,
   His wife could eat no lean,
And so between them both, you see,
   They licked the platter clean.

DOCTOR FOSTER

Doctor Foster went to Gloucester
In a shower of rain;
He stepped in a puddle,
Right up to his middle,
And never went there again.

YANKEE DOODLE

Yankee Doodle came to town,
   Riding on a pony,
He stuck a feather in his cap
   And called it macaroni.

40

TO THE RAIN

Rain, rain, go away,
Come again another day,
Little Johnny wants to play.
Rain, rain, go to Spain,
Never show your face again.

STAR LIGHT

Star light, star bright,
First star I see tonight,
I wish I may, I wish I might,
Have the wish I wish tonight.

JACK HORNER

Little Jack Horner
Sat in the corner,
Eating his Christmas pie;
He put in his thumb,
And pulled out a plum,
And said, What a good boy am I!

LITTLE MISS MUFFET

Little Miss Muffet
Sat on a tuffet,
Eating her curds and whey;
There came a big spider,
Who sat down beside her
And frightened Miss Muffet away.

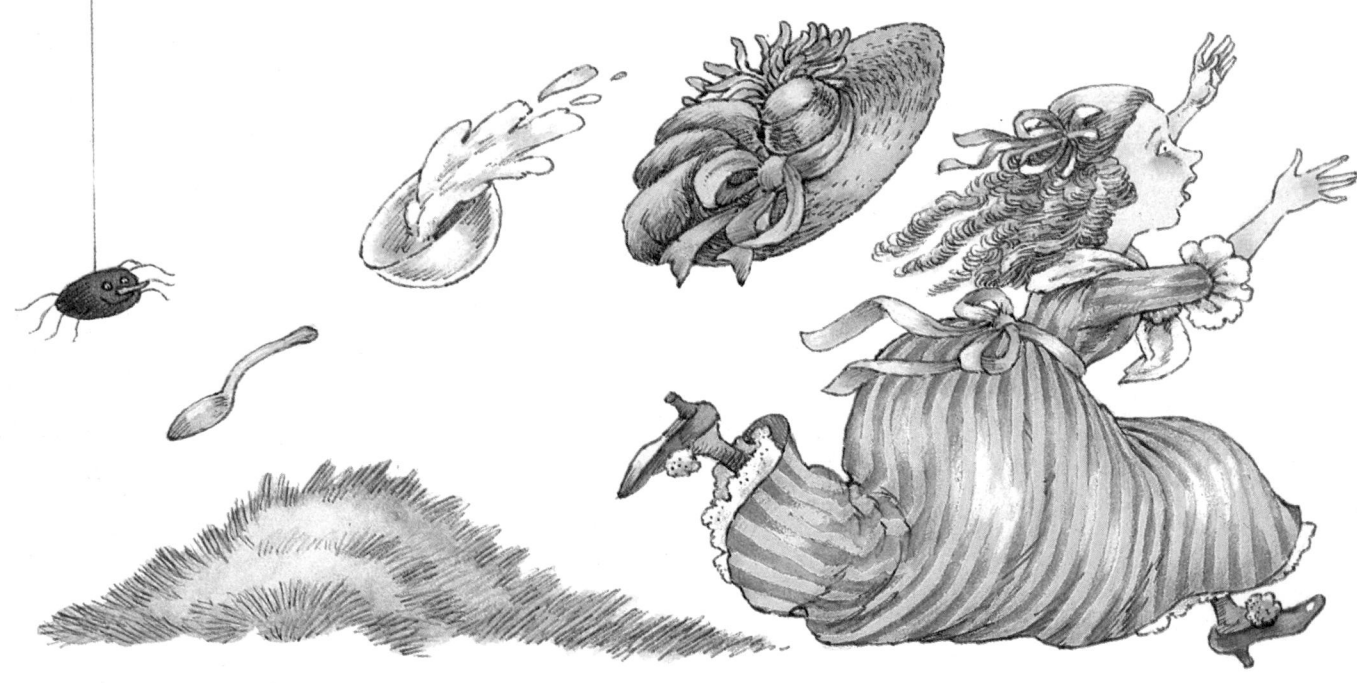

THREE MEN IN A TUB

Rub-a-dub-dub,
Three men in a tub,
And how do you think they got there?
The butcher, the baker,
The candlestick-maker,
They all jumped out of a rotten potato,
'Twas enough to make a man stare.

TO MARKET

To market, to market, to buy a fat pig,
Home again, home again, jiggety-jig;

To market, to market, to buy a fat hog,
Home again, home again, jiggety-jog.

IPSEY WIPSEY

Ipsey Wipsey spider,
    Climbing up the spout;
Down came the rain
    And washed the spider out;
Out came the sunshine
    And dried up all the rain;
Ipsey Wipsey spider,
    Climbing up again.

GOOSE FEATHERS

Cackle, cackle, Mother Goose,
Have you any feathers loose?
Truly have I, pretty fellow,
Half enough to fill a pillow.
Here are quills, take one or two,
And down to make a bed for you.

TO THE SNAIL

Snail, snail, put out your horns,
And I'll give you bread and barley corns.

THE OLD WOMAN IN A SHOE

There was an old woman who lived in a shoe;
She had so many children she didn't know what to do.
She gave them some broth without any bread;
Then whipped them all soundly and put them to bed.

ONE, TWO

1, 2,
Buckle my shoe;

3, 4,
Knock at the door;

5, 6,
Pick up sticks;

7, 8,
Lay them straight;

9, 10,
A big fat hen;

11, 12
Dig and delve;

13, 14,
Maids a-courting;

15, 16,
Maids in the kitchen;

17, 18,
Maids a-waiting;

19, 20,
My plate's empty.

I SAW A SHIP A-SAILING

I saw a ship a-sailing,
   A-sailing on the sea,
And oh, but it was laden
   With pretty things for thee!

There were comfits in the cabin,
   And apples in the hold;
The sails were made of silk,
   And the masts were made of gold.

The four-and-twenty sailors,
   That stood between the decks,
Were four-and-twenty white mice
   With chains about their necks.

The captain was a duck
   With a packet on his back,
And when the ship began to move
   The captain said, Quack! Quack!

THE MILKMAID

Little maid, pretty maid,
    Whither goest thou?
Down to the meadow
    To milk my cow.
Shall I go with thee?
    No, not now.
When I send for thee,
    Then come thou.

POLLY

Polly put the kettle on,
Polly put the kettle on,
Polly put the kettle on,
    We'll all have tea.

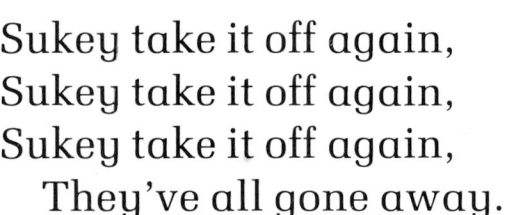

Sukey take it off again,
Sukey take it off again,
Sukey take it off again,
    They've all gone away.

TEN O'CLOCK SCHOLAR

A diller, a dollar,
A ten o'clock scholar,
What makes you come so soon?
You used to come at ten o'clock,
But now you come at noon.

ONE MISTY, MOISTY MORNING

One misty, moisty morning,
  When cloudy was the weather,
There I met an old man
  Clothed all in leather.

He began to compliment,
  And I began to grin,
How do you do, and how do you do,
  And how do you do again?

SEE-SAW, MARGERY DAW

See-saw, Margery Daw,
Jacky shall have a new master;
He shall have but a penny a day,
Because he can't work any faster.

THE HOUSE THAT JACK BUILT

This is the house
that Jack built.

This is the malt
That lay in the house
that Jack built.

This is the rat,
That ate the malt
That lay in the house
that Jack built.

This is the cat,
That killed the rat,
That ate the malt
That lay in the house
that Jack built.

This is the dog,
That worried the cat,
That killed the rat,
That ate the malt
That lay in the house
that Jack built.

This is the cow
    with the crumpled horn,
That tossed the dog,
That worried the cat,
That killed the rat,
That ate the malt
That lay in the house
    that Jack built.

This is the maiden all forlorn,
That milked the cow
    with the crumpled horn,
That tossed the dog,
That worried the cat,
That killed the rat,
That ate the malt
That lay in the house
    that Jack built.

This is the man all tattered
    and torn,
That kissed the maiden
    all forlorn,
That milked the cow
    with the crumpled horn,
That tossed the dog,
That worried the cat,
That killed the rat,
That ate the malt
That lay in the house
    that Jack built.

This is the priest all shaven and shorn,
That married the man
    all tattered and torn,
That kissed the maiden all forlorn,
That milked the cow
    with the crumpled horn,
That tossed the dog,
That worried the cat,
That killed the rat,
That ate the malt
That lay in the house
    that Jack built.

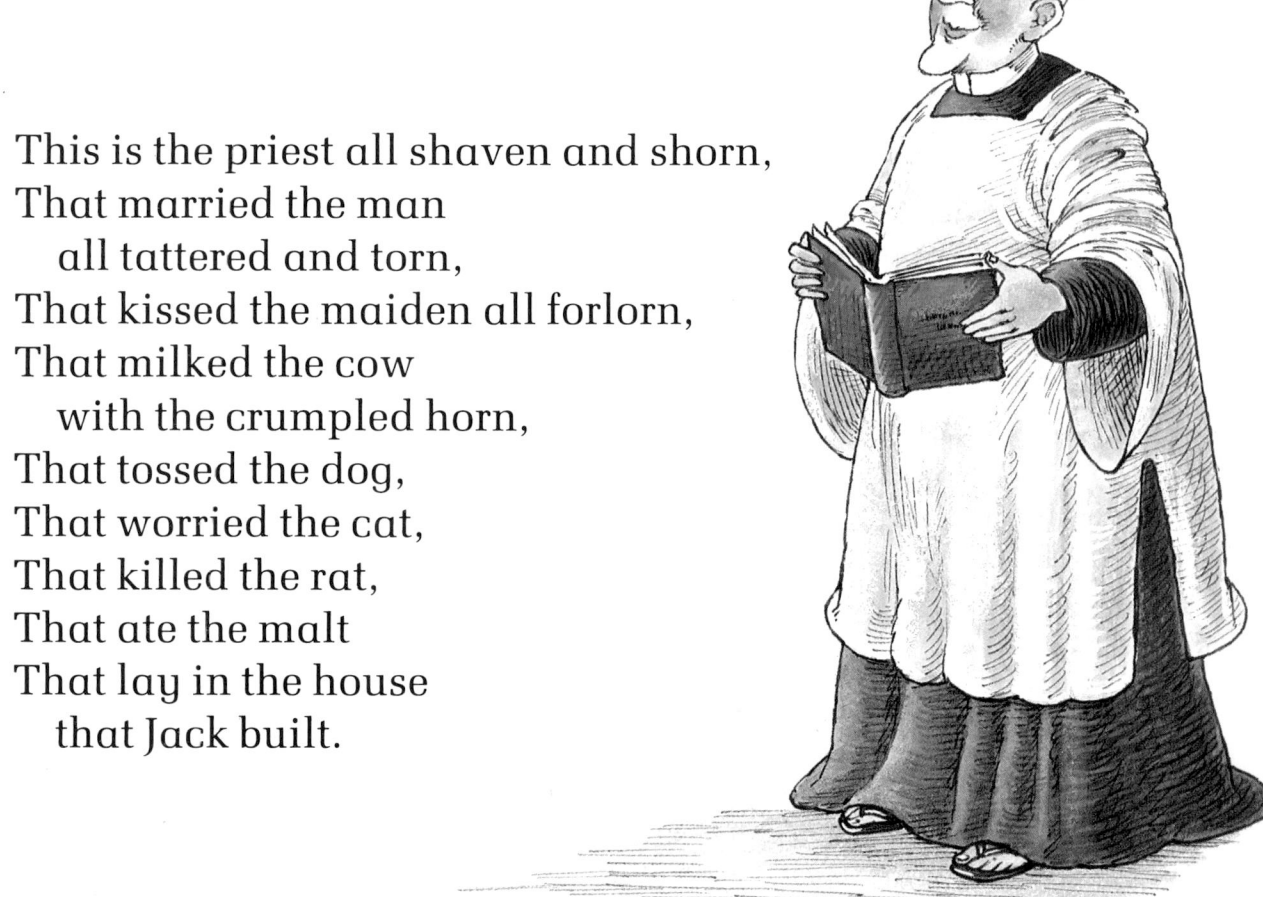

This is the cock
   that crowed in the morn,
That waked the priest
   all shaven and shorn,
That married the man
   all tattered and torn,
That kissed the maiden
   all forlorn,
That milked the cow
   with the crumpled horn,
That tossed the dog,
That worried the cat,
That killed the rat,
That ate the malt
That lay in the house
   that Jack built.

This is the farmer sowing his corn,
That kept the cock that crowed in the morn,
That waked the priest all shaven and shorn,
That married the man all tattered and torn,
That kissed the maiden all forlorn,
That milked the cow with
    the crumpled horn,
That tossed the dog,
That worried the cat,
That killed the rat,
That ate the malt
That lay in the house
    that Jack built.

This is the horse and the hound and the horn,
That belonged to the farmer sowing his corn,
That kept the cock that crowed in the morn,
That waked the priest all shaven and shorn,
That married the man all tattered and torn,
That kissed the maiden all forlorn,
That milked the cow with
    the crumpled horn,
That tossed the dog,
That worried the cat,
That killed the rat,
That ate the malt
That lay in the house
    that Jack built.

THE KEY OF THE KINGDOM

This is the key of the kingdom.
In that kingdom is a city,
In that city is a town,
In that town there is a street,
In that street there winds a lane,
In that lane there is a yard,
In that yard there is a house,
In that house there waits a room,
In that room there is a bed,
On that bed there is a basket,
   A basket of flowers.

Flowers in the basket,
Basket on the bed,
Bed in the chamber,
Chamber in the house,
House in the weedy yard,
Yard in the winding lane,
Lane in the broad street,
Street in the high town,
Town in the city,
City in the kingdom:
   This is the key of the kingdom.

THIS LITTLE PIG

This little pig went to market;
This little pig stayed at home;

This little pig had roast beef;
This little pig had none;
And this little pig cried, Wee-wee-wee!
    All the way home.

GOING TO ST IVES

As I was going to St Ives,
I met a man with seven wives;
Each wife had seven sacks,
Each sack had seven cats,
Each cat had seven kits:
Kits, cats, sacks, and wives,
How many were there going to St Ives?

(One or none)

64

GOOSEY GANDER

Goosey, goosey gander,
    Whither shall I wander?
Upstairs and downstairs
    And in my lady's chamber.
There I met an old man
    Who would not say his prayers,
I took him by the left leg
    And threw him down the stairs.

RIDE A COCK-HORSE

Ride a cock-horse to Banbury Cross,
To see a fine lady upon a white horse;
Rings on her fingers and bells on her toes,
She shall have music wherever she goes.

BOBBY SHAFTOE

Bobby Shaftoe's gone to sea,
Silver buckles on his knee;
He'll come back and marry me,
    Bonny Bobby Shaftoe.

Bobby Shaftoe's bright and fair,
Combing down his yellow hair,
He's my love for evermore,
    Bonny Bobby Shaftoe.

MY MOTHER SAID

My mother said, I never should
Play with the gypsies in the wood.
If I did, then she would say:
Naughty girl to disobey.
Your hair shan't curl and your shoes
   shan't shine,
You gypsy girl you shan't be mine.
And my father said that if I did,
He'd rap my head with the teapot lid.

COCK A DOODLE DOO

Cock a doodle doo!
My dame has lost her shoe,
My master's lost his fiddling stick
And knows not what to do.

Cock a doodle doo!
What is my dame to do?
Till master finds his fiddling stick
She'll dance without her shoe.

HANNAH BANTRY

Hannah Bantry,
In the pantry,
Gnawing at a mutton bone;
How she gnawed it,
How she clawed it,
When she found herself alone.

A NAIL

For want of a nail
   the shoe was lost,
For want of a shoe
   the horse was lost,
For want of a horse
   the rider was lost,
For want of a rider
   the battle was lost,
For want of a battle
   the kingdom was lost,
And all for the want
   of a horseshoe nail.

LITTLE TOMMY TITTLEMOUSE

Little Tommy Tittlemouse
Lived in a little house;
He caught fishes
In other men's ditches.

BABY BUNTING

Bye, baby bunting,
Daddy's gone a-hunting,
Gone to get a rabbit skin
To wrap the baby bunting in.

LITTLE BOY BLUE

Little Boy Blue,
  Come blow your horn.
The sheep's in the meadow,
  The cow's in the corn.
Where is the boy
  Who looks after the sheep?
He's under a haystack
  Fast asleep.
Will you wake him?
  No, not I,
For if I do,
  He's sure to cry.

TO THE LADYBIRD

Ladybird, ladybird,
    Fly away home,
Your house is on fire
    Your children all gone;
All but one,
    And her name is Ann,
And she has crept under
    The warming pan.

GREGORY GRIGGS

Gregory Griggs, Gregory Griggs,
Had twenty-seven different wigs.
He wore them up, he wore them down,
To please the people of the town;
He wore them east, he wore them west,
But he never could tell which he loved the best.

SIMPLE SIMON

Simple Simon met a pieman,
  Going to the fair;
Says Simple Simon to the pieman,
  Let me taste your ware.

Says the pieman to Simple Simon,
  Show me first your penny;
Says Simple Simon to the pieman,
  Indeed I have not any.

Simple Simon went a-fishing,
  For to catch a whale;
All the water he had got
  Was in his mother's pail.

Simple Simon went to look
  If plums grew on a thistle;
He pricked his fingers very much,
  Which made poor Simon whistle.

He went for water in a sieve
  But soon it all ran through;
And now poor Simple Simon
  Bids you all adieu.

THE CAT AND THE FIDDLE

Hey diddle, diddle,
The cat and the fiddle,
The cow jumped over the moon;
The little dog laughed
To see such sport,
And the dish ran away with the spoon.

SIX LITTLE MICE

Six little mice sat down to spin;
Pussy passed by and she peeped in.
What are you doing, my little men?
Weaving coats for gentlemen.
Shall I come in and cut off your threads?
No, no, Mistress Pussy, you'd bite off our heads.
Oh, no, I'll not; I'll help you to spin.
That may be so, but you don't come in.

TO THE MAGPIE

Magpie, magpie, flutter and flee,
Turn up your tail and good luck come to me.
One for sorrow, two for joy,
Three for a girl, four for a boy,
Five for silver, six for gold,
Seven for a secret ne'er to be told.

HODDLEY, PODDLEY

Hoddley, poddley, puddle and fogs,
Cats are to marry the poodle dogs;
Cats in blue jackets and dogs in red hats,
What will become of the mice and the rats?

THE BELLS OF LONDON

Oranges and lemons,
Say the bells of St Clement's.

You owe me five farthings,
Say the bells of St Martin's.

When will you pay me?
Say the bells of Old Bailey.

80

When I grow rich,
Say the bells of Shoreditch.

When will that be?
Say the bells of Stepney.

I'm sure I don't know,
Says the Great Bell of Bow.

Here comes the candle
to light you to bed,
Here comes the chopper,
to chop off your head.

CORPORAL BULL

Here's Corporal Bull
A strong hearty fellow,
Who not used to fighting
Set up a loud bellow.

BAA, BAA,
BLACK SHEEP

Baa, baa, black sheep,
   Have you any wool?
Yes, sir, yes, sir,
   Three bags full;
One for the master,
   And one for the dame,
And one for the little boy
   Who lives down the lane.

ROSES ARE RED

Roses are red,
Violets are blue,
Sugar is sweet
And so are you.

RING-A-RING O' ROSES

Ring-a-ring o' roses,
A pocket full of posies,
 A-tishoo! A-tishoo!
We all fall down.

MARY'S LAMB

Mary had a little lamb,
   Its fleece was white as snow;
And everywhere that Mary went
   The lamb was sure to go.

It followed her to school one day,
   That was against the rule;
It made the children laugh and play
   To see a lamb at school.

And so the teacher turned it out,
   But still it lingered near,
And waited patiently about
   Till Mary did appear.

Why does the lamb love Mary so?
   The eager children cry;
Why, Mary loves the lamb, you know,
   The teacher did reply.

HUMPTY DUMPTY

Humpty Dumpty sat on a wall,
Humpty Dumpty had a great fall;
   All the King's horses,
    And all the King's men,
Couldn't put Humpty together again.

COCK ROBIN

Who killed Cock Robin?
I, said the Sparrow,
With my bow and arrow,
I killed Cock Robin.

Who saw him die?
I, said the Fly,
With my little eye,
I saw him die.

Who caught his blood?
I, said the Fish,
With my little dish,
I caught his blood.

Who'll make his shroud?
I, said the Beetle,
With my thread and needle,
I'll make the shroud.

Who'll dig his grave?
I, said the Owl,
With my pick and shovel,
I'll dig his grave.

Who'll be the parson?
I, said the Rook,
With my little book,
I'll be the parson.

Who'll be the clerk?
I, said the Lark,
If it's not in the dark,
I'll be the clerk.

Who'll carry the link?
I, said the Linnet,
I'll fetch it in a minute,
I'll carry the link.

Who'll be chief mourner?
I, said the Dove,
I mourn for my love,
I'll be chief mourner.

Who'll carry the coffin?
I, said the Kite,
If it's not through the night
I'll carry the coffin.

Who'll bear the pall?
We, said the Wren,
Both the cock and the hen,
We'll bear the pall.

Who'll sing a psalm?
I, said the Thrush,
As she sat on a bush,
I'll sing a psalm.

Who'll toll the bell?
I, said the Bull,
Because I can pull,
I'll toll the bell.

All the birds of the air
Fell a-sighing and a-sobbing,
When they heard the bell toll
For poor Cock Robin.

THE MAN WITH NOUGHT

There was a man and he had nought,
    And robbers came to rob him;
He crept up to the chimney pot,
    And then they thought they had him.

But he got down on the other side,
    And then they could not find him;
He ran fourteen miles in fifteen days,
    And never looked behind him.

THE DONKEY

If I had a donkey that wouldn't go,
Would I beat him? Oh no, no.
I'd put him in the barn and give him some corn.
The best little donkey that ever was born.

88

OLD MOTHER SHUTTLE

Old Mother Shuttle,
Lived in a coal-scuttle
Along with her dog and her cat;
What they ate I can't tell,
But 'tis known very well
That not one of the party was fat.

Old Mother Shuttle
Scoured out her coal-scuttle,
And washed both her dog and her cat;
The cat scratched her nose,
So they came to hard blows,
And who was the gainer by that?

TOM, TOM

Tom, Tom, the piper's son,
Stole a pig and away did run;
   The pig was eat,
   And Tom was beat,
And Tom went howling
   down the street.

OLD WOMAN

There was an old woman
   Lived under a hill,
And if she's not gone
   She lives there still.

THE OWL

A wise old owl sat in an oak,
The more he heard the less he spoke;
The less he spoke the more he heard.
Why aren't we all like that wise old bird?

LUCY LOCKET

Lucy Locket lost her pocket,
  Kitty Fisher found it;
Not a penny was there in it,
  Only ribbon round it.

THREE LITTLE KITTENS

Three little kittens
They lost their mittens,
    And they began to cry,
Oh, Mother dear,
We sadly fear
Our mittens we have lost.
What! lost your mittens,
You naughty kittens!
Then you shall have no pie.
    Mee-ow, mee-ow, mee-ow.
No, you shall have no pie.

The three little kittens
They found their mittens,
    And they began to cry,
Oh, Mother dear,
See here, see here,
Our mittens we have found.
Put on your mittens,
You silly kittens,
And you shall have some pie.
    Purr-r, purr-r, purr-r,
Oh, let us have some pie.

The three little kittens
Put on their mittens
    And soon ate up the pie;
Oh, Mother dear,
We greatly fear
Our mittens we have soiled.
What! soiled your mittens,
You naughty kittens!
Then they began to sigh,
    Mee-ow, mee-ow, mee-ow,
Then they began to sigh.

The three little kittens
They washed their mittens,
    And hung them out to dry;
Oh, Mother dear,
Do you not hear,
Our mittens we have washed.
What! washed your mittens,
You good little kittens,
But I smell a rat close by.
    Mee-ow, mee-ow, mee-ow,
We smell a rat close by.

POLLY FLINDERS

Little Polly Flinders
Sat amongst the cinders,
Warming her pretty little toes;
Her mother came and caught her,
And whipped her little daughter
For spoiling her nice new clothes.

MY FATHER DIED

My father died a month ago
    And left me all his riches;
A feather bed, a wooden leg,
    And a pair of leather breeches;
A coffee pot without a spout,
    A cup without a handle,
A tobacco pipe without a lid,
    And half a farthing candle.

THE NORTH WIND

The north wind doth blow,
And we shall have snow,
And what will poor Robin do then,
    Poor thing?
He'll sit in a barn,
And keep himself warm,
And hide his head under his wing,
    Poor thing.

THE BEGGARS

Hark, hark, the dogs do bark,
    The beggars are coming to town;
Some in rags and some in jags,
    And one in a velvet gown.

TO BABYLON

How many miles to Babylon?
Three-score miles and ten.
Can I get there by candle-light?
Yes, and back again.
If your heels are nimble and light,
You may get there by candle-light.

DOCTOR FELL

I do not like thee, Doctor Fell,
The reason why I cannot tell;
But this I know, and know full well,
I do not like thee, Doctor Fell.

AN OLD WOMAN

There was an old woman tossed up in a basket,
Seventeen times as high as the moon;
And where was she going, I couldn't but ask it,
For in her hand she carried a broom.

Old woman, old woman, old woman, said I,
Where are you going to up so high?
To sweep the cobwebs off the sky!
Shall I go with you? Aye, by-and-by.

SING A SONG OF SIXPENCE

Sing a song of sixpence,
    A pocket full of rye;
Four-and-twenty blackbirds,
    Baked in a pie.

When the pie was opened,
    The birds began to sing;
Was not that a dainty dish,
    To set before the king?

The king was in his counting-house,
    Counting out his money;
The queen was in the parlour
    Eating bread and honey.

The maid was in the garden,
    Hanging out the clothes,
When down came a blackbird
    And pecked off her nose.

WHERE, OH WHERE

Oh where, oh where has my little dog gone?
    Oh where, oh where can he be?
With his ears cut short and his tail cut long,
    Oh where, oh where is he?

A MAN OF THESSALY

There was a man of Thessaly
    And he was wondrous wise,
He jumped into a bramble bush
    And scratched out both his eyes.
And when he saw his eyes were out,
    With all his might and main
He jumped into another bush
    And scratched them in again.

BANDY LEGS

As I was going to sell my eggs
I met a man with bandy legs,
Bandy legs and crooked toes;
I tripped up his heels, and he fell on his nose.

HOT CROSS BUNS

Hot cross buns! Hot cross buns!
One a penny, two a penny,
Hot cross buns!
If you have no daughters
Give them to your sons;
One a penny, two a penny
Hot cross buns.

OLD KING COLE

Old King Cole was a merry old soul,
And a merry old soul was he;
He called for his pipe and he called for his bowl,
And he called for his fiddlers three.

Every fiddler had a fiddle,
And a very fine fiddle had he;
Oh, there's none so rare as can compare
With King Cole and his fiddlers three.

THE GRAND OLD DUKE
OF YORK

Oh, the grand old Duke of York,
    He had ten thousand men;
He marched them up to the top of the hill,
    And he marched them down again.
And when they were up, they were up,
    And when they were down, they were down,
And when they were only half-way up,
    They were neither up nor down.

THE PIE

Who made the pie?
I did.

Who stole the pie?
He did.

Who found the pie?
She did.

Who ate the pie?
You did.

Who cried for pie?
We all did.

PETER, PETER

Peter, Peter, pumpkin eater,
Had a wife and couldn't keep her;
He put her in a pumpkin shell,
And there he kept her very well.

MY BLACK HEN

Hickety, pickety, my black hen,
She lays eggs for gentlemen;
Sometimes one, and sometimes ten,
Hickety, pickety, my black hen.

LITTLE BO-PEEP

Little Bo-peep has lost her sheep,
    And can't tell where to find them;
Leave them alone, and they'll come home,
    Bringing their tails behind them.

Little Bo-peep fell fast asleep,
    And dreamt she heard them bleating;
But when she awoke, she found it a joke,
    For they were still a-fleeting.

Then up she took her little crook,
  Determined for to find them;
She found them indeed, but it made her heart bleed
  For they'd left their tails behind them.

It happened one day, as Bo-peep did stray
  Into a meadow hard by,
There she espied their tails side by side,
  All hung on a tree to dry.

She heaved a sigh, and wiped her eye,
  And over the hillocks went rambling,
And tried what she could as a shepherdess should,
  To tack each again to its lambkin.

JACK-A-NORY

I'll tell you a story
About Jack-a-Nory,
And now my story's begun;
I'll tell you another
About Jack and his brother,
And now my story is done.

TO BED

To bed, to bed,
Says Sleepy-head;
Tarry a while, says Slow;
Put on the pan,
Says Greedy Nan,
We'll sup before we go.

THE JOLLY MILLER

There was a jolly miller once,
    Lived on the river Dee;
He worked and sang from morn till night,
    No lark more blithe than he.
And this the burden of his song
    Forever used to be,
I care for nobody, no, not I,
    If nobody cares for me.

THE LITTLE NUT TREE

I had a little nut tree,
  Nothing would it bear
But a silver nutmeg
  And a golden pear.
The king of Spain's daughter
  Came to visit me,
All for the sake
  Of my little nut tree.

DIDDLE, DIDDLE, DUMPLING

Diddle, diddle, dumpling, my son John,
Went to bed with his trousers on;
One shoe off, and one shoe on,
Diddle, diddle, dumpling, my son John.

TWINKLE, TWINKLE

Twinkle, twinkle, little star,
How I wonder what you are!
Up above the world so high,
Like a diamond in the sky.

THREE YOUNG RATS

Three young rats with black felt hats,
Three young ducks with new straw flats,
Three young dogs with curling tails,
Three young cats with demi-veils,
Went out to walk with two young pigs
In satin vests and sorrel wigs;
But suddenly it chanced to rain
And so they all went home again.

TERENCE McDIDDLER

Terence McDiddler,
The three-stringed fiddler,
Can charm, if you please,
The fish from the seas.

CHRISTMAS IS COMING

Christmas is coming,
The geese are getting fat,
Please to put a penny
In the old man's hat.
If you haven't got a penny,
A ha'penny will do;
If you haven't got a ha'penny,
Then God bless you!

GUNPOWDER PLOT

Please to remember
The fifth of November,
Gunpowder treason and plot;
I see no reason
Why gunpowder treason
Should ever be forgot.

PINS

See a pin and pick it up,
All the day you'll have good luck.
See a pin and let it lay,
Bad luck you'll have all the day.

IF WISHES
WERE
HORSES

If wishes were horses,
   Beggars would ride.
If turnips were watches,
   I would wear one by my side.
And if "ifs" and "ands" were pots and pans,
There'd be no work for tinkers!

THE QUEEN OF HEARTS

The Queen of Hearts
She made some tarts,
All on a summer's day;
The Knave of Hearts
He stole the tarts,
And took them clean away.

The King of Hearts
Called for the tarts,
And beat the knave full sore;
The Knave of Hearts
Brought back the tarts,
And vowed he'd steal no more.

PUSSY CAT, PUSSY CAT

Pussy cat, pussy cat,
   Where have you been?
I've been to London
   To look at the Queen.

Pussy cat, pussy cat,
   What did you there?
I frightened a little mouse
   Under her chair.